Dr. Rae Rivera

BYTE-SIZED LESSONS WITH ZOLA AND ZENA

Cyber Pups Keep You Safe

Adventures in internet safety with two cyber-savvy pups

WOODBRIDGE
PUBLISHERS

276 5th Avenue Suite 704 #944
New York, NY 10001

ISBN (Paperback)
ISBN (Hardback)
ISBN (eBook)

DEDICATION

To Zola —
My loyal friend, steadfast through every high and low.

Your gentle presence, boundless love, and unshakable spirit have been my constant comfort and inspiration.

You've taught me more about patience, trust, and unconditional love than any lesson could.

This book is dedicated to you—my heart, my old lady, my forever good girl.

CHAPTER 1: MEET THE CYBER PUPS

Zola is a senior American Bulldog. She is white with black spots, wears rounded glasses, and has a cybersecurity badge. She is calm, wise, and a bit of a mother hen. She wears a vest with authenticators and carries a laptop in her backpack.

Zena is a young, energetic, curious white English Bull Terrier with pointy ears. She wears a bright red cape and has a headset for her cyber missions. She has a backpack and a bone-shaped tablet with cyber stickers.

Zola and Zena's Mission:

i. Protect the dog park (and the internet) from sneaky cyber trouble.
ii. The setting is in a digital dog park where "data bones" are buried. There is a doghouse with a computer lab with "pawprint scanners" for authenticating into the computer. The park includes "malware mutts" and "phish cats" as villains.

CHAPTER 2: THE CASE OF THE TRICKY TREAT LINK

It was a sunny day, and Zena wagged her tail as she checked her "Pup Mail."

She barked, "Wow! A message that says 'Click here for free treats forever!'"

Zola peeked over her glasses. "Hmm... that smells phishy!"
"Phishy?" asked Zena. "But it says treats!"

Zola chuckled. "Not every link brings treats, little pup. Some bring trouble! Let's sniff out the tricky ones together!"
Zena clicks the link anyway in the suspicious email promising unlimited dog treats. Unfortunately, it was a phishing link sent by one of the phish cats, and Zena accidentally downloaded malware.

Zola stepped in and ran an anti-virus program to get rid of the malware. Zola then teaches Zena how to spot phishing tricks.

Sem: treats4u@dogmail.net
Dear Pooch,
To good to be true offer
Urgent language
Free treats !!
Click here!
www.tasty-treats.dog
Fake URL
Fake URL

CHAPTER 2 Activities: "TheTreat Trap: Spot the Phishy Link!"

Objective: Teach kids how to recognize phishing scams by identifying suspicious messages, links, and offers.

Skills Practiced: Online safety, reading comprehension, and decision-making

Activity 1: Sniff Out the Scam!

Instructions: Read each message and indicate whether it is SAFE or PHISHY.

Message:	Safe or Phishy?
"Hey Zena! Click here to claim free treats!"	
"Hi Zena, Zola invited you to a dog park game you joined last week."	
"Update your password by clicking this link—NOW!"	
"Congrats, Zena! You won a prize! Just give your name and doghouse address!"	
"New fetch level unlocked! Tap here to play with your friends."	

Smells Safe!
Smells Phishy!
You won a year of free snacks!
Enter your password to keep playing
Click to see Zola's new photo
Join your classmate's dog park group

Activity 2: Zola's "Smell Test" Sorting Game

Match the bones on page 12 to the correct Dog Bowl.

Zola's Big Lesson Takeway

If it asks for something personal (like passwords, addresses, or money), it goes in the Phishy bowl!

COMPUTER
LAB
Username
Password
LOG IN

CHAPTER 3: PASSWORD PAWTECTION

Zola told Zena, "Our doghouse has a super lock—just like your online accounts!

But if your password's weak, a sneaky raccoon 'hacker' might sneak in!"

Zena wagged her tail, "Then I'll make the strongest password ever!"

Zola smiled, "Let's practice how to make passwords that even a cyber-cat can't crack!"

Zola explains to Zena how passwords are secret codes for accessing online accounts.

They protect our information and the data bones' locations from the malware mutt and phish cat villains. If they get our password, they can steal our data bones.

A password is like a key to our doghouse. What makes them strong?

- How long they are. The longer the better.
- Using a mix of upper case, lower case, numbers, and symbols.
- Avoid using obvious information about you: name, birthdays, using "password" or "123456", family names, etc.

Eager to try to type in the password to access their computer lab, Zola tells Zena Not so fast. There is more to protecting our data bones than just a password. Zola shows Zena the pawprint scanner.

Zola explains that the best way to protect online accounts is by using more than one access measure or multi-factor authentication, such as a pawprint scanner in combination with a password. That way, if your password is stolen, they still need to have your pawprint to unlock the account.

Login

CHAPTER 3 Activities: "Lock the Doghouse! Zola's Password Pawtection Game"

Objective: Teach children how to create strong, safe passwords using memorable patterns and creative thinking.

Skills Practiced: Cyber awareness, critical thinking, creativity.

Activity 1: Build-A-Password Challenge

Instructions: Kids fill in the blanks using Zola's password-building rules.

Zola's Password Formula	Example
1. Start with a favorite thing	Bone
2. Add a special number	27
3. Add a symbol	!
4. Mix in UPPER and lower letters	BoNe27!
5. Don't forget — no real names or birthdays!	Zena123

Now You Try It!
Write your paw-some password below:
My Strong Password:___________________________________

Activity 2: "Guess That Password!" Game

Kids circle the strongest one.
1.Password: zola123
2.Password: ILoveBones!
3.Password: B@rkStrong27!

Zena barks: A hint. It's the hardest to guess and uses symbols, numbers, and letters!"

Zola says: "A strong password keeps your info safe in the doghouse AND online!"

Activity 3: Color & Create

Kids draw Zola guarding a doghouse with a big lock symbol.

Kids can color the lock, write their password formula inside, and decorate it with stickers or symbols that remind them of strength (like shields, bones, or stars).

Zola's Big Lesson Takeaway

"A strong password is your first defense—It keeps bad bugs from climbing the fence!"

- Use letters, numbers, and symbols
- Keep it secret—don't share it!
- Change it sometimes to stay safe online

COMPUTER
LAB
★★★★★

CHAPTER 4: STRANGER DANGER ONLINE

Zena was playing her favorite online fetch game when a new pup named "CoolDog99" sent her a message:
"Hey Zena! Wanna meet at the park? I know where you live—it's by the big red hydrant!"
Zena's ears perked up. Should she answer back? Before she could type, Zola barked. "Stop right there, little pup! Let's figure this out together."

Zola explains why it is important to be cautious about who you speak to online. You do not always know the person on the other end. You should never share any personal information online that might identify you in the future.

Some specific threats include:

- It can lead to cyberbullying.
- Inappropriate content can be shared.
- Can lead to the sharing of personal information.
- Can lead to being targeted to do something that you should not.

CHAPTER 4 Activities: "Friend or Phony? Zena's Online Game Challenge!"

Objective: Help kids learn to identify safe online friends and understand when to say "no" to strangers online.

Skills Practiced: Critical thinking, online safety awareness, and decision-making

Activity 1: Friend or Phony?

Kids read several short messages and indicate whether it's from a "Friend" or a "Phony."

Messages:

1. "Hey Zena! Want to play fetch like yesterday?" Friend or Phony
2. "Hi! I'm a pup you don't know, but I have a secret game for you." Friend or Phony
3. "Can you tell me your password so we can match?" Friend or Phony
4. "Nice score, Zena! I'll see you in class tomorrow. Friend or Phony
5. "I'm your friend's cousin, tell me your address so I can send treats!" Friend or Phony

Activity 2: Find the safe path to get safely to Zena.

- Safe path signs: "Ask a grown-up." "Keep info private." "Play with real friends."
- Danger path signs: "Share your password." "Click unknown link." "Meet a mystery pup."

Ask a grown-up
Share password
Keep info private
Click unknown link
Play with real friends
Meet a mystery pup
Zena
A
B
C

Zola's Big Lesson Takeaway

"Not every pup online is who they say! Keep your info private—don't give it away!"

- Only chat with friends you know in real life
- Ask an adult if something feels weird or scary
- Never share your name. address. or password online

Share your password
Click unknown link
Meet a mystery pup

CHAPTER 5: POSTING FOR PAWS

Zena was wagging her tail with pride! She just posted a selfie in front of her shiny doghouse.

"Look, Zola! I got five paws-up already!" Zena barked.
Zola squinted. "Zena, do you see what's behind you?"
"My doghouse?" Zena asked.
"Yes—and your address! Oh, pup! You just told the whole internet where you live!"
Zena's ears drooped. "Oh no..."
"Don't worry," Zola smiled. "Let's learn how to post safely, step by step."
Zola explained to Zena that it is important as a young pup to protect all your personal information. She went on to share a complete checklist to follow before posting anything online.

- Never share personal details: home, address, phone, school name, or birthday.
- Disable location services on phone and social media apps or ask an adult to help.
- Never share your passwords with anyone.
- Always ask yourself: Would you want a parent or teacher to see it?
- Do not post photos of others without their permission.

Following this checklist will keep your personal information protected online and allow you to still enjoy social media.

CHAPTER 5: Activity: The Safe Selfie Challenge!

Objective: Teach children to think before posting photos and to understand what personal information should be kept private.

Skills Practiced: Digital citizenship, privacy awareness, and visual safety spotting

Activity 1: The Safe Selfie Challenge!

Instructions: Below are four "Puppy Posts." Indicate the ones that are SAFE and or ones that SHARE TOO MUCH INFO!

Mark: ✓ Safe or X Not Safe

Puppy Post

"Just chilling in my yard at 123 Bone Street!" (photo shows house number)

"Having fun at the park with Zola!" (photo shows trees and ball)

"My new collar tag says: Zena – call me at 555-1234!"

"Movie night with my best buddy!" (photo shows couch and popcorn)

Activity 2: Zola's Privacy Checklist

Check off what Zena should hide before posting:

- ☐ Address number
- ☐ School name
- ☐ Phone number
- ☐ License plate
- ☐ Family names
- ☐ Favorite toy
- ☐ Treats

Zola's Big Lesson Takeaway Poem:

"Before you post, take time to see,
What's in the pic for all to see!
Keep your name and home away,
And you'll post smart every day!"

COMPUTER
LAB
A
B
Bark-Book
Apps

CHAPTER 6: PRIVACY PAWS

Zena wagged her tail as he scrolled through her Bark-Book page. "Look, Zola! I made my page public so every dog can see my new squeaky toy!"

Zola tilted her head. "Public, huh? That means even sneaky squirrels and unknown pups can see your posts!"

Zena gasped. "Even the mailman dog?"

"Yup!" Zola barked. "Let's fix those settings so only your real friends can see."

Together, they clicked through buttons, making the page safer one paw at a time.

Zola explained to Zena the importance of privacy settings and what they do. Privacy settings control how your personal data and online content are shared with others. They help protect your security and your online reputation. Specifically, they:

- Control access to information.
- Help manage content visibility.
- Limit ad tracking.
- Shape your online reputation.

Zola explained the different settings and what they mean.

Public -> everyone can see, even if they are not your friend.

Friends Only -> only people that are on your friends list.

Only Me -> only you can see this content.

So, when you post, make certain to review the privacy settings and make sure it is appropriate for the post.

CHAPTER 6 Activities: "Privacy Paws Patrol!"

Objective: Help children understand what privacy settings do, why they're important, and how to decide what to share online.

Skills Practiced: Online safety, decision-making, and responsible digital use

Activity 1: Who Can See Zena's Page?

Instructions: Match each Bark-Book setting to the right group that can see Zena's posts.

Setting	Who Can See?	
Public	Zola, Daisy, and pups Zena know	✓
Friends Only	Just Zena herself	✓
Only Me	Everyone, even strangers	X

Activity 2: Privacy Paw Patrol Checklist

Help Zena make sure her page is safe!

Check off what Zena should do:

- ☐ Make posts visible to Friends Only
- ☐ Turn off location sharing
- ☐ Use a nickname instead of a full name
- ☐ Hide personal info (like home address)
- ☐ Share happy moments, not private details
- ☐ Use a strong password. Zola helped her make

Activity 3: "Fix the Feed!" Sorting Game

Put an "X" in the correct column for each item to mark as Safe to Share or Keep Private

Safe to Share	List of items	Keep Private
	Zena's new frisbee photo	
	Zena's home address	
	Zola's birthday party	
	Zena's phone number	
	Funny paw-print cookies	
	School name	
	Park playdate with friends	
	Zena's password	

Zola's Big Lesson Takeaway Poem

"When you share online, take care each day,
To keep your private stuff tucked away!
Friends you trust can wag along,
With privacy paws, you'll stay strong!"

COMPUTER
LAB
ZENA

CHAPTER 7: THE BUG IN THE BONE APP

It was a sunny morning; Zena found a shiny new app called "Bone Bonanza!"
"It gives free treats for every click!" she barked.
Zola raised an eyebrow. "Free treats? That sounds too good to be true, pup."
Suddenly—BZZZT! —Zena's tablet started acting strange. Her games froze, and her doggy photos disappeared!
"Oh no! A bug got into the Bone App!" Zola said.
"How do we stop it?" Zena yelped.
"With safe downloads and updates, of course," Zola smiled. "Let's go bug-hunting!"
After Zola removed the bug from Zena's tablet, she shared what to do to prevent this from happening again. Zola's recommendations are:

- Only download apps from official stores such as Google Play Store or Apple Store.
- Beware of exaggerated claims about the app.
- Apply bug updates immediately.
- Limit app permissions.
- Clear app cache and data when the app acts weird.

Zena put her tablet down and joined Zola to patrol the dog park to make sure the data bones were still secure

CHAPTER 7 Activities: "Zola's Bug Hunt!"

Objective: Teach children how to recognize safe apps, the importance of software updates, and how to avoid "buggy" or fake apps.

Skills Practiced: Digital safety, critical thinking, app recognition

Activity 1: “Spot the Sneaky App!”

Instructions:
Mark each App as ✓Safe, or X Not Safe in the right column.

App Icon	Description	Safe or Not Safe?
Bone Bonanza	Promises unlimited treats if you share your password.	
PupPix	Let's you share photos with friends you know.	
FetchRunner	Downloaded from the official PetPlay Store.	
Free Bones Forever	Asks for location, photos, and passwords.	

Activity 2: "Patch That Pup!"

Objective: Teach kids about keeping devices updated.

Instructions:
Zola's tablet has missing "update patches"!
Check the box for each reason updates are important:

- ☐ Fix bugs that make devices act weird
- ☐ Keep sneaky hackers out
- ☐ Add new fun features
- ☐ Make apps run faster

Activity 2: "Safe or Risky Sorting Game"

Put an "X" in the correct column for each item to mark if it is a Safe Download or Risky Download:

Safe Download	Download Items	Risky Download
	From the official app store	
	From a mystery link	
	Has good reviews	
	Asks for camera access only when needed	
	No reviews or all 1-star	
	Updated regularly	
	Asks for your password or personal info	
	Outdated or unknown source	

Bonus Rhyme: Zola's Bug-Free Beat

"If an app looks weird or new,
Ask before you click—think it through!
Keep your system fresh and bright,
Updates help you sleep at night!"

COMPUTER LAB
Username
*****
LOG IN

CHAPTER 8: ZOLA'S CYBER CHECKLIST

Zena wagged her tail proudly as she looked at her glowing screen. "Zola! I've learned so much about being safe online—no tricky links, no sharing my address, and always strong passwords!"
Zola grinned. "You sure have, kiddo. Sounds like you're ready to make your own Cyber Checklist!"

Zena barked happily. "Let's make it tail-wagging approved!"
Zena started to create her Cyber Checklist on her tablet. The list includes:

- Always use strong passwords and never share them with anyone.
- Do not share personal information online.
- Use privacy settings on all apps and social media sites.
- Do not click links in emails, especially if they seem fishy.
- Be aware of people you do not know when online and do not talk or share any information with them.
- It is okay to share online, just make sure to share safely.

CHAPTER 8 Activities: “Zena’s Cyber Checklist Challenge!”

Objective: Reinforce all previous lessons—password safety, privacy, phishing, stranger danger, and safe sharing—through a fun, creative checklist and reflection activity.

Skills Practiced: Responsible digital behavior, self-assessment, reflection, and recall.

Activity 1: Zena's Cyber Checklist – "Paw Print It Off!"

Instructions: Help Zena check off each safety step she's mastered. Color in the paw next to each rule you already follow!

Cyber Checklist Items	Zena's Cyber Checklist
I use a strong password with letters, numbers, and symbols	
I never click on links that look suspicious or offer "free treats."	
I only talk to friends I know in real life online.	
I keep my personal info private (no addresses, schools, or phone numbers).	
I ask an adult if I'm unsure about something online. I update my apps and devices to stay safe.	
I think before I post—if Zola wouldn't bark it, I don't post it!	
I use privacy settings to control who sees my posts.	

Once all paws are checked, write your name under:
"Official Member of the Cyber Pups Patrol!"

Activity 2: Design Your Own "Cyber Pup Poster"

Materials: Crayons or markers, paper or poster
Instructions: Draw Zena and Zola holding a big cyber safety poster with your favorite online safety tip.

Examples of slogans:

- "Think Before You Click!"
- "Pause Before You Post!"
- "Strong Passwords Keep Paws Protected!"

Encourage creativity—add paw prints, bones, and computer screens with smiley faces!

Activity 3: Zena's Cyber Scenarios Game

Instructions: Read each scenario and in the right column indicate if it is safe "SAFE" or "NOT SAFE"

Scenario	Safe? Or Not Safe
Zena gets a message from "PuppyFan123" asking for her address.	
Zola updates her tablet when it says "New Security Patch Available."	
Zena posts a photo showing her dog tag with her name and phone number.	
Zola uses a password that's "Zola123."	
Zena tells her parent before joining a new dog game online.	

Zola's Closing Poem: "Cyber Smart, Start to Bark!"

"When you're online, be cool and kind,
Keep your safety in mind!
Click with care, and think things through,
A cyber-smart pup's the best kind of you!"

STAY CYBER
SAFE ONLINE

ACKNOWLEDGEMENTS

This book would not have been possible without the encouragement and inspiration of so many wonderful people.

To Zola, whose loyal companionship and quiet strength carried me through every challenge — your spirit fills each page with heart and purpose.

To Zena, whose playful curiosity reminds us all to keep learning, exploring, and protecting what matters most.

To my family and friends, thank you for believing in this vision and cheering me on through every late night and rewrite.

To the educators, parents, and young readers who bring these lessons to life — your passion for teaching digital citizenship and online safety makes the world a safer, kinder place.

And to everyone working to create a brighter, safer digital future for the next generation — this book is for you.

ABOUT THE AUTHOR

Dr. Rae Rivera has been a cybersecurity professional for over 15 years. Most of her time has been spent in global security education and talent development, catalyzing transformative learning environments that foster career mobility, employee retention, and organizational resilience. Her expertise is anchored in the strategic design and delivery of training programs, integrated with risk intelligence and advanced phishing and awareness campaigns to safeguard and enhance corporate ecosystems. Her leadership is characterized by a steadfast commitment to diversity, equity, and inclusion, ensuring that each educational initiative promotes a culture of continuous growth and learning. Through leveraging cutting-edge technology and innovative methodologies, She's been instrumental in upskilling talent pools and aligning educational strategies with business objectives, resulting in significant cost reductions and heightened security postures. Her career is a testament to developing impactful certification programs and steering crossfunctional teams towards surpassing industry standards in cybersecurity, privacy, and access management. At the heart of her professional journey is a deep-seated passion for nurturing inclusive, knowledgeable, and agile learning communities, ready to tackle the challenges of tomorrow.

BYTE-SIZED LESSONS WITH ZOLA AND ZENA

Join ***Zola and Zena***—two curious friends who explore the digital world one byte at a time! Through colorful stories, fun challenges, and real-world examples, young readers learn how to protect themselves and become confident digital citizens.

This engaging book makes cybersecurity simple, fun, and empowering for kids. Each "byte-sized" lesson introduces an essential safety concept with relatable scenarios and easy-to-follow tips and fun activities. Perfect for classrooms, parents, and after-school programs, ***Byte-Sized Lessons with Zola & Zena*** builds lifelong skills for safe, responsible, and respectful online behavior.

Readers will learn to understand basic cybersecurity and online safety concepts, identify safe vs. unsafe online behaviors, develop digital citizenship skills—responsibility, respect, and privacy, recognize the importance of passwords, privacy settings, and secure communication, and build confidence in navigating the digital world safely.

With ***Zola and Zena*** as their guides, students will laugh, learn, and level up their online smarts—one byte at a time!

About the Author

Dr. Rae Rivera has been a cybersecurity professional for over 15 years. Most of her time has been spent in global security education and talent development, catalyzing transformative learning environments that foster career mobility, employee retention, and organizational resilience. Her expertise is anchored in the strategic design and delivery of training programs, integrated with risk intelligence and advanced phishing and awareness campaigns to safeguard and enhance corporate ecosystems. Her career is a testament to developing impactful certification and education programs and steering cross-functional teams towards surpassing industry standards in cybersecurity, privacy, and access management.

Dr. Rae Rivera

www.ingramcontent.com/pod-product-compliance
Lightning Source LLC
LaVergne TN
LVHW070857210926
848482LV00016B/964
* 9 7 9 8 2 9 5 5 5 0 3 5 5 *